THE AWAKENING HEART

VOLUME II

JAMYANG TENPHEL

This book first published 2025
Timeless Awareness Publications
www.timeless-awareness.com

© 2025 by Jamyang Tenphel
Cover design: Jamyang Tenphel
Interior design: Pema Düddul

978-0-6458571-8-4
First Edition
National Library of Australia Cataloguing-in-
Publication entry:

Tenphel, Jamyang. 1976–
The Awakening Heart: Volume 2/Jamyang Tenphel
978-0-6458571-8-4 (pbk.)
Non-Fiction—Philosophy & Religion
Non-Fiction—Self Help and Personal Development

DEDICATION

I dedicate this book to my extraordinary Master, Kyabje Togden Amtrin. I would also like to dedicate it to all of the Awakened Ones, the Dakinis and Dharmapalas, and to all of the Lineage Masters of the Dzogchen Semde tradition— those remembered and those forgotten. I owe you everything.

Last, and most certainly not least, I would like to dedicate this to Lama Dudjom Pema Düddul, whose constant support means more than I can say.
Thank you. I love you all.

CONTENTS

ACKNOWLEDGEMENTS

Once again, I would like to acknowledge all First Nations people, especially the indigenous peoples of Australia. I would also like to acknowledge all of my Dharma siblings who have been marginalised due to their race, ethnicity, gender, sexuality, and differences in ability; or for any other reason. I see you, I hear you, and I love you all very much.

May all beings, without exception, awaken and be free!

FOREWORD

It is with deep gratitude and joy that I introduce *The Awakening Heart: Volume Two*. The first volume has served as a lantern for many seekers, illuminating the path of practice with clarity, warmth, and profound insight. For this, I offer my heartfelt thanks to Jamyang and all those who have used the book to walk alongside us in the Dharma.

Buddhist practice is not merely an intellectual exercise or a solitary pursuit; it is a living, breathing journey of transformation that touches every aspect of our lives. The teachings in this new book were born from Jamyang's dedicated exploration of the path and his earnest desire to provide practical guidance for those navigating the joys and challenges of spiritual practice.

This second volume of pith instructions has been drawn from the last six years of Jamyang's retreat, especially the last two years. In preparing this volume, Jamyang has been mindful of the evolving needs of Dharma practitioners in this fast-paced, digitally interconnected world. While the core teachings remain timeless and unchanged, Jamyang has sought to clarify commonly misunderstood ideas and include instructions to support readers in grounding their practice amidst the complexities of modern life. This is why the bulk of the pith instructions in this book are focused on Dzogchen and the nature of mind, which is the perfect approach for modern times.

Above all, this book is an offering of mettā, loving-kindness. It is Jamyang's aspiration, and my own, that it serves as a guide for Awakening to the boundless clarity and compassion that lie at the heart of our true nature. May it inspire you to meet each moment with courage, wisdom, and tenderness, and may it lead you closer to the ultimate freedom that is the birthright of all beings.

Lama Dudjom Pema Düddul
Amtrin Dudjom Ling, Australia
January 2025

Kyabje Togden Amtrin

THE
AWAKENING
HEART

108 Pith Instructions
For Buddhist Practice

Volume Two

INTRODUCTION

Pith instructions are an offering to our true nature, our Buddha Nature, pristine Awareness itself. We offer it by reciting it gently and easily a few times over, and then resting in silent stillness. The heart knows what to do with it. You just relax, surrender to the pith instruction and rest in stillness. Do not hold on to the pith instruction, cling to it, or try to suck the life out of it. Let it breathe. Surrender and relax. Don't contemplate it on the cushion. Let resting in silent stillness do all the work, whether it be in shamatha, sky gazing, or corpse pose.

A pith instruction is an offering to the heart, not a weapon to use against the mind. Offer the pith instruction to your heart and ask for nothing in return. Once offered to the heart in this way, by simply speaking it aloud a few times gently and with no expectations of getting anything in return, we just rest and allow it to undermine the self in its own way and in its own time. Trust this process. It will work. Be patient.

Just as water breaks through the toughest stone without effort, just like wind can reshape the mightiest trees completely naturally, so too pith instructions, in conjunction with stillness, undermine the dualistic mind, naturally and effortlessly, inevitably leading one to the state of Awakening.

So surrender, relax, and soften the heart.

There is no freedom without surrender.

SECTION ONE

The greatest conduct is joy.
The greatest purification is joy.
The greatest accumulation is joy.
Joy is the mother of Immeasurable Love and
Compassion –
the mother of Awakening itself.
~ Kyabje Togden Amtrin, given directly to Jamyang Tenphel

ཨེ།

Happiness is a simple thing,
arrived at by simple means.

Be quiet, open your heart, and listen.

How else will you find out what others truly need?

Joy's natural radiance is Awareness itself.

Each and every moment is full of the potential to recognise this.

Love is the only response to injustice.

Love is the only response to prejudice.

Love is the only response to hatred and fear.

Love is the only thing that will free us from this mess that we are all in together.

Just love.

Relax.

Relax into joy,

Relax into love,

Relax into compassion,

Relax into equanimity,

Relax into freedom!

Just relax.

To bring joy to another's heart is the greatest gift we can give.

It is a moment of freedom from the suffering of this world.

This is Bodhisattva work.

To give freely and without concern
undermines samsara completely.
The self knows this.

All the stories we tell ourselves

about who and what we are

are pure fabrications.

So, what does that make us?

The mind is empty,

neither good nor bad.

If it is neither good nor bad, nor any other findable thing,

then what is it?

Pure Awareness.

That is all.

There is no meeting and no parting when it comes to the Buddha Nature.

No separation, not ever.

And so, in the same way, there is no meeting, no parting, and no separation from the Guru, even once they die.

The Guru, like our Buddha Nature, has always been there, and will always be there – unborn, undying, unending.

The Guru is our innate perfection, the Buddha within us all, and therefore is who we truly are, have always been, and will always be.

To rest in joy's natural radiance is to rest in the natural state itself.

There is nothing beyond this.

Abiding in perfect simplicity.

Inconceivable and Immeasurable.

This is the Path of Joy and Ease.

Relax and delight effortlessly in joy's natural radiance,

just as you would effortlessly delight

in the sun's natural radiance

on a cold winter's day.

Just having the wish to practice the Dharma and help others is enough,

especially when you are very sick and fatigued.

The profound potency of resting in this simple heartfelt aspiration

is enough to liberate you from all disturbing emotions in this very moment.

Rest deeply, and have confidence in this.

Don't take yourself too seriously.

You don't really exist.

When you sit down to meditate,

do so without expectations, hopes or fears.

Do not cling to thoughts or non-thought.

Do not cling to pleasant or unpleasant sensations.

Do not cling to clarity or distractions.

Just simply sit, and let it all come and go, just as it is.

Stop trying to get somewhere.

There is nowhere to go.

The problems we have with others

are often just problems we have with ourselves.

Anger and yearning, guilt and shame, and feeling unworthy –

These will never be resolved by externalizing them,

but only by looking directly at them, into them and through them.

This will reveal their empty and untrue nature.

Impermanence, ultimately, folds time and space back in on itself until it comes right back to this present nowness, Timeless Awareness. No future. No past.

Impermanence leads back to no time, no space, only perfect absolute nowness.

Time and space are totally empty and have no substance at all.

Rest in stillness, and know this for yourself.

One of the greatest lessons the Buddha's teachings give us is how to adapt – how to use ingenuity in the face of challenges to adapt to the constantly changing conditions of our existence. If we don't learn to adapt, then the constant flux of reality will cause us to suffer greatly.

If we learn to be flexible and adaptable, our suffering will diminish considerably.

To accept changing circumstances and adapt accordingly – this is bringing the aspects of wisdom and skilful means together to navigate this conditioned reality with a minimum of suffering.

The empty nature of this reality we live in

means that things are constantly changing,

in constant flux.

The fact that all things are empty

means that we all have the capacity to change with this
flux.

Thoughts arise from emptiness,

abide in emptiness,

and dissolve back into emptiness, the Natural State.

This is the true nature of reality.

Thoughts don't intend to be grasped, clung to, or acted upon.

They simply arise, like wisps of smoke, out of the Dharmadhatu, the ground of emptiness, and float through our "minds".

We see these wisps of illusion and rush to hold onto them.

But what if we just allowed the illusory wisps to arise and dissolve back into emptiness, the Natural State, without believing they are real and holding on with all our might?

Would we not be free?

The only commitment that the Dharma requires of you is to look into the nature and condition of your mind.

Just look.
That is all.

Don't attribute anything more to your experience than is already there naturally.

Don't give any more importance to the breath than it just being a breath.

Don't attribute any more importance to experiences than what they simply are.

Leave everything that arises, internally and externally, naked and as it is.

Don't layer extra meanings on top of things and then cling to and create a narrative around them.

Leave it all be.

This is the Dzogchen view, to let everything arise and dissolve as it is.

No matter how high and exalted our experiences may be,

as long as we continue to differentiate between ourselves and others,

we are as much in samsara as any other being.

Feeling love and showing kindness to others is the antidote to anxiety and sadness.

Love, Bodhicitta, destroys the self.

Anxiety and sadness come from strong self-grasping and fear.

Love is self-less.

Anxiety withers in its presence.

The joy derived from true practice exceeds ordinary pleasures and entertainments infinitely!

The peace that comes from deep stillness during meditation.

The bliss-joy that arises in the heart when Bodhicitta blazes forth.

The vast, spacious, relaxed openness that comes from dissolving the self.

These make worldly pleasures seem utterly insignificant and worthless.

So, turn your mind away from ordinariness and towards the Dharma!

The conceptual, dualistic mind is conditioned, or pre-programmed, with all of these formulaic responses to every situation, emotion, feeling, and thought that arises.

Through our regular contemplation practice, we change these conditioned responses to help us handle difficult situations and disturbing emotions more easily, and with more composure, equanimity and kindness to others and ourselves.

It takes time, of course, so patience and perseverance is required, but we have to start somewhere, or we'll always be slaves to our thoughts, feelings and external situations.

Calm abiding meditation (Shamata) is about proving the emptiness of the mind.

The mind can go from turbulent to calm and back again,

thus proving it is impermanent and insubstantial –

empty of any lasting qualities or states, and dependent on causes and conditions.

Shamata gives us confidence that the mind is flexible and changeable, and "enlightenable"!

True renunciation

is completely letting go of the past and the future.

It is not an external act.

True renunciation takes place in the heart.

SECTION TWO

When we abide in the state of Dzogchen there is absolutely no wish to harm any living being or oneself. There is only Bodhicitta, boundless love and compassion without discrimination. Therefore, when we adopt the five precepts in our training in the Great Perfection we are not adopting a rigid oppressive code of living, we are simply turning our hearts toward home and our natural condition.

~ Kyabje Togden Amtrin, given directly to Jamyang Tenphel

ཁ

Opening the heart begins with simple joy
and culminates in luminous wonder.

Compassion is meeting people as they are.

Right now,

in this very moment,

not who they might have been in the past.

The hardest practice in the Dharma

is to do nothing

and just be with yourself.

Genuine heart-felt joy *is* our true nature.

It has all of the factors of Awakening within it,

yet it is so deceptively simple that we overlook it,

and continue to search for more.

For those with devotion,

life-stories of great Dharma practitioners

are vessels of liberating blessings.

The outer words hold meaning

that only the heart can truly know.

Loving-kindness and compassion
are our true nature.
One does not need to cultivate
that which is our natural condition.
So, relax freely in whatever arises
and remain there.

The Dzogchen path
is entirely about heart.

Dzogchen requires no effort.
It is the state of absolute effortlessness;
and in this state of effortlessness,
everything is indescribably perfect.
Just as it is.

The self makes us feel as though

we are the centre of the universe.

In effortless relaxation we see this clearly,

and clearly see it is not true.

No effort equals no self.

The self is behind all effort.

For as long as our practice is based on effort,
we will never be free.

To be utterly effortless is to be utterly free.

The self is behind all of our ambitions and desires.

With the self liberated,

we realise that there is nothing to achieve

and nothing to attain.

There is only limitless rest.

All beings are composite in nature;

neither good nor bad in essence;

and all are equally deserving of love and compassion.

All thoughts, feelings, and emotions

are composite in nature;

neither good nor bad in essence;

and all are equally Pristine Awareness.

We are all born with the same innate potential to Awaken.

If anyone makes you feel that this is not true, anyone at all,

you must politely turn your back and walk away from them.

Nothing is more important

than having confidence in your Buddha Nature.

Devotion is the key

that unlocks everything you need

to Awaken.

There is only this moment

There is only this moment

There is only this moment

There is only this moment

There is only this moment

There is only this moment

There is only this moment

There is only this moment

There is only this moment

There is only this moment

There is only this moment

and nothing more.

The seeds of Awakening exist within us already.

Water them with great joy.

Nourish them with great love.

Tend to them with great compassion.

And allow them to ripen

in the atmosphere of perfect equanimity.

Karma relies on time to exist,

and only has its effects in relative reality.

In Timeless Awareness, ultimate reality,

there is no more cause and effect,

only limitless freedom.

There is no "normal" or "abnormal",
whatever is, *is*.
On any given day,
in any given moment,
just let it be and relax.

When you have tried all of the therapies,

remedies and distractions

that samsara has to offer,

and have still found no peace or contentment,

it is time to offer yourself to the Dharma –

the ultimate medicine that cures all suffering.

To rest in our natural condition

is to rest in whatever *is*,

in this very moment

without trying to block it,

enhance it,

or act on it in any way.

Simply rest limitlessly in what is.

There is no past, present or future.

No distance, near or far.

No centre or edge.

No now or then.

No time or space at all.

No you, no me, no us, no them.

There is only Awareness

and nothing more.

The seed creates the fruit.

For as long as we use relative methods

involving words and form

we will remain in the relative state of samsara.

The real *Tummo* is the blazing bliss of devotion.

Let this liberating bliss

blaze in your hearts

and burn away all thoughts of self and other,

this and that,

right and wrong,

good and bad.

When we gaze into the sky and a bird flies past,

do we get annoyed, upset, or distressed?

Of course not.

In the same way

allow thoughts to drift through our minds harmlessly

and just let them be as they are.

Nothing to do.

Trying to know that which cannot be known,

is like trying to suck nectar from a stone.

Give up trying and relax completely.

There is nothing to get.

With a light heart,

unburdened by the wish to accomplish anything at all;

joy, love, compassion and equanimity

accompany us everywhere.

SECTION THREE

Sky-gazing is resting in spaciousness
And corpse pose is resting in stillness;
Together they encompass
the entire Dzogchen path.
~ Kyabje Togden Amtrin, given directly to Jamyang
Tenphel

ཨ

Lie like a corpse;
silent,
still,
without object
or objective.

Look at the sky;
silent,
still,
Without object
or objective.

This is Dzogchen Semde,
The Primordial Path of Effortless Simplicity.

To rest in the natural radiance of whatever occurs
is the supreme and unsurpassable Dharma.

Clinging to experiences,

good or bad,

is samsara.

One cannot truly understand the depths of misery that samsara brings

until one experiences the relief from it –

the complete and total relief of relaxing into one's true nature,

our true home.

After tasting this,

one's commitment to Awakening,

for oneself and others,

becomes absolute.

How could it not?

There are only two things to remember

when engaging in the profoundly liberating practice of sky-gazing.

There is nothing to do

and there is nothing to get.

Leave the mind in its place

Just as it is

Unbound and untethered

Free to move, like the wind

We are our thoughts.

Our thoughts are none other than the self.

When we no longer believe that our thoughts are real and true,

we no longer believe that the self is real and true.

Without a solid foundation in the Dharma,

and a daily meditation practice,

experiences will come and go

like dreams

and leave nothing of worth behind.

Worse still,

they simply become a source of pride and greater delusion.

Consistent practice is required until we abide in the Immeasurables

continuously and effortlessly.

When one's mind becomes suffused with Dharma

Everything becomes of benefit

Stop looking for certainty.

There is none.

Stop searching for permanence.

It cannot be found.

What you truly seek

is already within you.

If you wish to quench your thirst for understanding,
put down your books
and sit in stillness.

We are not separate.

The practice I do for myself

is the practice I do for others.

And the practice I do for others

is the practice that I do for myself.

The heart's true language
is that of the Four Immeasurables;
not the language of doctrine
and philosophies.

True practice occurs in those moments

of pure and simple joy,

love and compassion,

wonder and awe.

These are the moments that will lead you to freedom.

Follow them.

Dreams are just thoughts.

Thoughts are just dreams,

nothing more.

The past is dead.

You cannot purify it.

There is nothing to purify.

It is gone.

Move on.

You cannot change the past.

All there is, is now.

Just now.

There are two ways into the state of the Great Perfection –

total love and total devotion.

Total love requires you to love all beings,

equally and completely.

Devotion only requires you to love one.

The greatest paradox in all of the Dharma

is that by doing absolutely nothing

the most extraordinary something

happens

all by itself.

Everyone wants to be something;
until you realise that being something
is what keeps you in samsara.

There is no self

There is only now

In sky-gazing there are no good or bad sessions.

No good or bad experiences,

no good or bad thoughts or feelings.

No good or bad at all!

In sky-gazing all becomes equal naturally.

And all becomes One.

Ask yourself:

Am I just performing Buddhism

or am I actually practicing it?

Am I just presenting a fabricated simulacrum

of what I think a Buddhist practitioner is,

for appearance's sake,

or do I truly wish to be free from all suffering?

Guru Rinpoche's pure realm

is found in the centre of your own heart.

It is the luminous Awareness

that is inseparable from your True Nature.

It is within and without you

at all times.

We are it and it is us.

Pure realms are nothing more or less

than our own pure perception.

Soften into devotion.

Let simple love and gratitude to the Awakened Ones carry you home to freedom.

Let the soothing winds of Awareness
blow through the vast meadows of mind,
free and unhindered.

Keep one eye on the path

and one eye on the top of the mountain.

This way you will not lose sight

of where you are now,

and where you are going.

Nor will you set up camp on the path

and become stuck,

or gaze solely at the end, and stumble into pitfalls

Guru Yoga is the one practice that accomplishes all in one lifetime.

Free from requiring the practitioner to traverse through all of the levels and stages of other methods, Guru Yoga accomplishes Shamata, Vipassana, Trekcho and Togal in one great wondrous leap.

This supreme practice of open-hearted simplicity, free from contrivance and fabrication, is spontaneous presence itself.

Guru Yoga is liberation in one lifetime.

True patience

is the absence

of waiting for anything to happen at all.

SECTION FOUR

The Guiding Lights Of Awareness

We can recognise Awareness, our True Nature, through the experiences of immeasurable joy, love, compassion and equanimity. These are the guiding lights that take us home to full Awakening. These are the luminous states that open our hearts and lead us to, and allow us to rest in, perfect ease and freedom.

Awareness is inexplicable, unfathomable, and cannot be known in any ordinary sense or by any ordinary means. This nondual state of Awareness can only be experienced directly. Words and form are useless in knowing Awareness. However, our heart, being Awareness itself, recognizes itself in the expressions of great joy, love, compassion and equanimity.

The Four Immeasurables are incontrovertible, you either have them or you do not. There is nothing to discuss and nothing to debate. It is entirely about experience. Our own direct experience.

Follow these four immeasurable states home to the state of the Buddhas. Follow these and you cannot go wrong. Experiences such as dreams, visions, non-thought, bliss states and so on may lead you astray, but these four wondrous states never will. This is how you know you are on the right track, no matter what Dharma path you are on – Sutra, Mahayana, Vajrayana or Dzogchen.

~ Kyabje Togden Amtrin, given directly to Jamyang Tenphel

ༀ

In order to Awaken
we must let go
of everything we know,
and everything we believe.

True rest is not an act of the body
but an act of the mind.
It is in true rest that realisation dawns.

Every single concept or belief that we adopt and cling to now

is just one more concept or belief that we will need to let go of in the future.

Be mindful of this and remain simple.

Time and space do not truly exist.

Therefore, neither death nor distance

are a barrier between us and those abiding

in Timeless Awareness.

Devotion completely dissolves

this perceived separation,

and places us in a state of union

with the Ultimate Guru:

Awareness itself.

Do not cling to the outer face or form of the Guru.

Your own true face is Awareness itself.

How can we settle into the natural state

if we continue to apply effort?

The natural state requires no embellishments of the mind,

it is perfection itself.

Have confidence in this.

If you wish to visit Lord Guru Padma's pure realm,

You need do nothing more than open your eyes

and you are there!

This luminous reality,

inseparable from the Great Guru himself,

Arises from nowhere other than your own heart!

In naked simplicity

there is nothing to look back upon

and nothing to look forward to.

In non-activity,

all hopes and fears self-liberate spontaneously.

Truly letting go

relies on supreme confidence

in your Buddha Nature.

The Buddhas, Gurus, deities and dakinis
abide in the centre of your own heart.
Look nowhere else.

Without joy,

the miseries of samsara

will taint everything you do;

whether it be your ordinary activities

or your Dharma practice.

Without joy,

dissatisfaction will be all-pervasive.

Relax and rest in the state of unknowing.
It will do you the world of good.

When the self is liberated

and our individual Awareness (*rigpa*)

merges with the ocean of Awareness (*Dharmadhatu*)

final freedom is found.

Do not settle for nice experiences,

they are just entertainments.

Do not be led around by the nose,

like a poor old yak,

enslaved by mind's appearances.

Let the dualistic apparitions

come and go;

clinging to nothing,

investing in nothing,

identifying with nothing.

When you lose all taste for coming and going,

learning and knowing,

doing and doing,

then you can finally begin to rest

in your True Nature.

AH!

By becoming a conduit for the Buddhas,

we become truly able to see what beings need and how to give it to them.

Without offering ourselves entirely in this way,

our benefit to others will always be limited.

When we abide in Awareness

we become the perfect conduit to benefit all beings.

Gently relax your grip on the past and its events.

Relax your grip on the present and what you think of as right and wrong.

Relax your grip on the future and what you hope it looks like.

Relax so entirely that only this moment exists,

and nothing more.

Dzogchen is primordial,

beginningless.

It belongs to no religion or tradition.

It is every single living being's birthright.

Our right to freedom!

You are not your body.

You are not your thoughts.

You are not your feelings.

You are Awareness.

One with All.

Where is this mind

that you wish to cleanse and purify?

I have not been able to find it.

The essence of all disturbing emotions
is sky-like Awareness –
empty, open and vast.

Awareness cannot be produced by any thought.

It cannot be expressed by any words.

It cannot be created by any action.

It cannot be found in any place.

The mind is a complete fabrication

that can never go beyond

the conditioned parameters of the dualistic state.

To understand this deeply

is to take your first step toward Liberation.

Relax the gaze

and allow empty appearances

to self-liberate

into empty luminosity.

The inner luminosity

reflects the outer luminosity.

The outer luminosity

reflects the inner luminosity.

And it all begins with opening the heart.

All thoughts and feelings arise
from the great ocean of fundamental Awareness,
and thus, by nature, are Awareness itself.

When water is taken from the ocean
it does not become something else.
It remains water, always.
Just so, Awareness remains Awareness
no matter what form it takes.

Relax in this understanding and rest limitlessly.

All of the seeking and learning,
supplicating and visualising,
accumulating and purifying;
all to simply recognise
the fundamental goodness
that has been within us all along.

I know now, with absolute certainty,

that one does not need physical and cognitive wellness

to be free from samsara.

Through Guru Yoga, and the blessings of the Guru,

one can be placed in the state beyond hope and fear,

and rest in the primordial perfection innate to us all.

I bow to the Gurus!

I bow to Kyabje Togden Amtrin!

Let go of words.

They can never come close to expressing

the true heart of the Dharma.

Be simple with the Dharma.

Don't overcomplicate things.

Awakening should be a joyful experience.

I know this is not what you have been told.

Hold the Dharma lightly.

Practice simply.

Do not cling ...

Do not cling ...

Let go.

Jamyang Tenphel with Kyabje Togden Amtrin (2004)

ABOUT THE AUTHOR

Rigdzin Jamyang Tenphel is an Australian-born Buddhist practitioner and founding Co-Director of *Pristine Awareness: Foundation for Buddhist Practice*. He discovered the Dharma in 1995 at the age of 19 and then studied and practiced in Australia and India for the next decade, primarily in the Tibetan tradition. Jamyang took monastic ordination in 2001. He handed back his monastic robes in 2005 and in the same year took white robe ordination in the Dudjom tradition with Ngakpa Karma Lhundup Rinpoche. Jamyang's Guru is the late Kyabje Togden Amtrin, a highly revered yogi of the Drukpa Kagyu lineage from Khampagar Monastery in Eastern Tibet. Despite a debilitating and sometimes life-threatening chronic illness of over 20 years' duration, Jamyang has maintained his meditation practice, using his sick bed as his retreat place. He went into retreat at the beginning of 2019, and has no fixed end date. Jamyang has a degree in Social Welfare and is author of *The Awakening Heart: Volume One*. He is co-author, along with Pema Düddul, of *Resting in Stillness*, a book about meditation, compassion and the nature of the mind. Jamyang was given the blessing to teach Dharma in 2006. Since then, this blessing has been extended to him by a number of masters.

If you enjoyed this book, please leave a review at Amazon.com.

Other Books by Jamyang Tenphel
The Awakening Heart: Volume One, Timeless Awareness Publications, 2023
Resting in Stillness by Jamyang Tenphel, & Pema Düddul, Jalu Publications, 2020.

Recent Books from Timeless Awareness Publications:

Natural Presence: Concise Advice on Buddhist Practice by Pema Düddul, 2024
Luminous Awareness: A Guidebook to Awakening in Life and in Death by Pema Düddul, 2022.

If this book has inspired you to practice according to the pith instruction tradition go to:
www.pristine-awareness.org
www.youtube.com/@pristine.awareness

Note: If you are interested, audio instructions on how to use pith instructions in meditation practice can be found here:
https://youtu.be/TrScDjTV6AU?si=vvdmpXpyldsfbOXn